IMAGES
of America

CENTRALIA

The steeple of St. Ignatius was the last part of this historic church to be torn down. Following the crash, two birds flew out from inside the steeple's cross.

IMAGES
of America

CENTRALIA

Deryl B. Johnson

ARCADIA
PUBLISHING

Published by Arcadia Publishing
Charleston, South Carolina

Library of Congress Catalog Card Number: 2004105633

For all general information contact Arcadia Publishing at:
Telephone 843-853-2070
Fax 843-853-0044
E-mail sales@arcadiapublishing.com
For customer service and orders:
Toll-Free 1-888-313-2665

Visit us on the Internet at www.arcadiapublishing.com

To the current and former residents of Centralia,
who have brought life to this town for almost 140 years and
who have taught me the meaning of community, and to my parents,
Frank and Patricia Johnson, who have taught me the meaning of family.

In this photograph of Sarah Yeager's former house, note how the faux chimneys on the side of the house disguise the steel beams supporting the walls.

CONTENTS

ACKNOWLEDGMENTS

My thanks to the many people who lent their support in researching this project. The following people provided photographs: Vanessa Bucher, Thomas Dempsey, Anne Marie Devine, Shari Garman, Andrew Gray and family, Tom Kufta, John J. Lokitis Jr., Tom Hill, Owen McGinley, Harry "Doc" Moleski, Raymond Reilley, Albina Schickley, Don Spieless, Jerry "Slovie" Wolchansky, and Joe Yeager.

This book also includes anecdotes courtesy of the following: Academy Sporting Goods and Luncheonette of Mount Carmel and Academy "Beauties," Bernie Yasenchak, Bill Malley, Thomas Dempsey, Molly's of Locus Gap, Sarah Isally (McDonnell) Noga, Tom Symons, Harry "Doc" Moleski, Molly Darrah, Chester Kulesa, Lamar and Lanna Mervine, Stephanie Whyne, Jim Cleary, Tommy Fedock, Charlie Strausser, Jack Darrah, Tiny, Margarite, Sammy, Fritz, Charlotte, Sonny, Soupy, Patrick Campbell, Eric McKeever, John Hardines, Thomas Hynoski, Walter Simons, Sarah Yeager, Anne Marie Devine, Andrew Gray and family, Joseph Maczka, Pete Kenenitz, Owen McGinley, Jerry "Slovie" Wysochansky, Mount Carmel Public Library, the *News-Item*, and the members of Centralia Fire Company No. 1.

INTRODUCTION

For more than 40 years, a fire has been burning in Centralia, Pennsylvania. In 1962, Centralia was a small mining community of 1,600 people. On an unseasonably warm March night in 1998, I knocked on the door of Mayor Lamar Mervine, and he and his wife, Lanna, generously invited me into their home. I had met Lamar briefly more than seven months earlier when I began researching and writing a play about this intriguing underground mine fire. I was fascinated by the fact that a town in my adopted state of Pennsylvania stood over an underground mine fire—a fire burning for almost 40 years! I was also fascinated that, despite a government buyout and a declaration of eminent domain by Gov. Bob Casey, some residents of this community had refused to relocate. Originally, I had ventured to Centralia like so many reporters and visitors looking for evidence of a fire and seeking the answer to one question: Why would anyone live above a mine fire? The answer is simple. It is very hard to leave a place where your neighbors are just like family, a place where your mother is everybody's mother.

Today, we hear stories of communities fighting to have many important building declared historical landmarks. We read of people striving to keep their favorite church from merging with another, then resulting in its closure and demolition. But now imagine that every building you have ever known is destroyed. Imagine that every family you were raised with, and often times your grandparents were raised with, have been forced to move away from each other. This is what has happened to Centralia.

Centralia is a place where the Mammoth Store, Alexander Rea, Demokoski's Tap Room, Capt. Jack Crawford, the Sisters of Immaculate Heart of Mary, skinny dipping in the Lily, Sousa's, Hubert Eicher High School, Jack Micginley's tavern, the American Legion building, sleigh riding down Buck's Patch, the Old Burkle, Stutz's Funeral Home, Father Phelan's St. Patrick's Day minstrel shows, the Zeisloft station, and Coddington's Gulf station are but images and memories of a town nearly wiped away from the face of the earth.

In this book, I try to capture some of these images and stories of one of Pennsylvania's most famous and infamous towns. My play *Centralia* first premiered at Kutztown University of Pennsylvania in 1998. Since then, I have continued to collect tales and photographs from Centralia's colorful past. The generosity of people associated with the town's past and present has been overwhelming. This book affords me a chance to give back to the countless number of people who have shared their reflections on this unusual but extremely giving community. I would like readers to know that all the author profits from this book will be given to the Centralia Fire Department and to the Library of Mount Carmel, Pennsylvania.

I hope that you find here a bit of the passion and spirit that burns beneath this famous town—a warmth that is generated by the humanity and zest for life that this community once had and will always remain in the minds and hearts of those who knew her.

This book is divided into six chapters. Chapter 1 focuses on the origins of the town and its development through the early 1960s, when the fire began. Chapter 2 centers on the major driving force in the economic development of the town—the coal industry. Home, school, and church life is featured in chapter 3. The rise and fall of Centralia's most enduring icons and its largest congregation, St. Ignatius Roman Catholic Church, is the subject of chapter 4. Chapter 5 presents some of the images from the demolition of the town and the physical effects of the fire itself. The final chapter centers on Centralia as it appeared in 2004.

—Deryl B. Johnson
June 2004

A Brief Historical Timeline

1841: Bull's Head Tavern opens.

1855: Alexander W. Rea, engineer and agent for the Locust Mountain Coal & Iron Company, surveys the town into streets and lots.

1866: The borough of Centralia is officially established.

1869: In April, services for St. Ignatius Roman Catholic Church begin.

1908: In December, a severe fire in Centralia wipes out an entire block on Locust Avenue. Forty-two buildings are destroyed, and 34 families (150 people) are left homeless.

1918: Nearly 10 percent of Centralia's population dies from Spanish influenza.

1948: The second-worst airline disaster in U.S. history before 1950 occurs. A DC-6 crashes in Mid Valley. Rescue efforts are headquartered in Centralia.

1962: In May, the fire begins.

1962–1978: The state and federal governments expend $3.3 million to control the fire.

1984: Congress appropriates $42 million for voluntary acquisition and relocation due to dangers caused by the fire.

1985–1991: Residents are moved, and 545 homes and businesses are acquired. Condemnation procedures are initiated to acquire properties and relocate the remaining residents of Centralia. Route 61 is rerouted indefinitely due to fire damage.

1993–1994: County and state supreme courts rule against property owner objections to relocation and mineral rights ownership. St. Ignatius is demolished during Thanksgiving weekend. In April, warning signs are posted.

2004: Fewer than 20 buildings and 10 people remain in Centralia.

This P. H. Loeper photograph was taken on December 4, 1908. After a fire destroyed an entire block on Locust Avenue, more than 150 people had to be cared for with only $4,000 worth of insurance and $75,000 worth of damage. A rumor spread that the fire was deliberately set by the coal company to get at the rich vein directly under the town.

One

BEFORE THE FIRE

Centralia's history began in 1804 with the opening of the Red Tavern. In 1842, after the discovery of coal in the area, the Locust Mountain Coal & Iron Company opened the Mine Run Colliery. Soon, there were the Locust Run, Coal Ridge, Hazel Dell, Centralia, and Continental Collieries in the area.

In 1841, Jonathan Foust built Bull's Head Tavern, the first building on the site of Centralia. Alexander W. Rea, an engineer at the Locust Mountain Colliery, named the town and laid out the streets. Rea said he chose the name "Centralia" because it was the center of everything, of people coming together. Rea even suggested and donated the land for St. Ignatius Catholic Church; however, he did not live long enough to see the church open. Rea's was one of the first and most visible murders linked to the infamous Molly Maguire scandal.

During the 1860s and 1870s, the coal regions of Pennsylvania expanded dramatically. In this period, mine workers increased from just over 25,000 to 56,000. The low-paid work was extremely difficult, long, and dangerous. Most of the new mine workers were immigrants. Almost a third of the immigrants were Irish and Roman Catholic, while many of the railroad and mine owners were Scottish (such as Rea) and Anglican. The tension between ethnic class, religion, and social class created great tensions.

Three important groups representing the mine workers emerged at this time: the Workers Benevolent Association, the Ancient Order of Hibernians (an organization associated with Roman Catholicism), and a secret Irish organization known as the Molly Maguires. There is much controversy and much written about the role of the Molly Maguires. During this period, rampant crime occurred. Some 260 murders were recorded in neighboring Schuylkill County between 1860 and 1890. The Mollies were blamed for this violence. Some believe that the Mollies were guilty, while others claim that the Mollies were framed by the owners of the mines who feared that the members of the Mollies and the leaders of the Ancient Order of Hibernians and the Workers Benevolent Association would organize the mine workers into unions. The Alexander Rea murder and the trial of the alleged murderer was one of the biggest stories during this tumultuous time in Pennsylvania history. Patrick Hester was arrested, released, and re-arrested and tried 10 years after the crime. He was eventually found guilty and hung, but this trial and the true role of the Molly Maguires still evoke controversy today.

Centralia has seen its share of tragedies. Numerous fires during the late 19th and early 20th centuries devastated large parts of the town. Since Centralia rests on what is called the Mammoth Vein, many believed that these fires were deliberately set. After the most brutal fire, in 1908, much of the coal under the destroyed homes was removed. However, the coal company filled in the earth poorly, and many of the rebuilt homes suffered from extreme settling. Before the current fire forced the tearing down of homes on Locust Avenue, it was not uncommon to see bowed walls in many of those rebuilt homes.

An influenza outbreak in 1918 killed more than 10 percent of the entire town's population. In 1948, the second-worst national plane disaster pre-1950 occurred outside of Centralia. The famous crash killed Broadway producer Earl Carroll and Beryl Wallace, wife of comedian Jack Oakey. After the plane crash, one body went unclaimed by family members in New York. The town supplied the funeral and burial plot in their own Odd Fellows cemetery. More than 50 years after the crash, former residents of Centralia still put flowers on the grave of a man nobody ever met.

Despite these tragedies, the demise of the coal industry, and the resulting loss of jobs due to the closing of every colliery in the area during the 1950s and 1960s, Centralia endured. It was not until 1962 that disaster truly struck. While trash burned in a dump, an unknown vein of coal caught fire, took hold, and has been burning ever since.

In this chapter, you will see images from Centralia's colorful past. The images cover a period from 1870 through 1964.

This southward view shows the 400 block of Locust Avenue *c.* 1913.

This view looks north at the same intersection of downtown Centralia *c.* 1913.

In this 1906 photograph taken by P. H. Loeper of Ashland, we see how Centralia looked at the turn of the century. Many of the homes demolished in the 1980s and 1990s had stood

Publ. by P. H. Loeper, Ashland Pa.

for over 100 years.

The Mammoth Company Store, owned by the Lehigh Valley Coal Company, was located on North Locust Avenue.

Dykes Hotel, seen here *c.* 1910, was the first veteran's facility in Centralia.

In this 1906 bird's-eye view, the steeple of St. Ignatius Catholic Church is barely visible in the center.

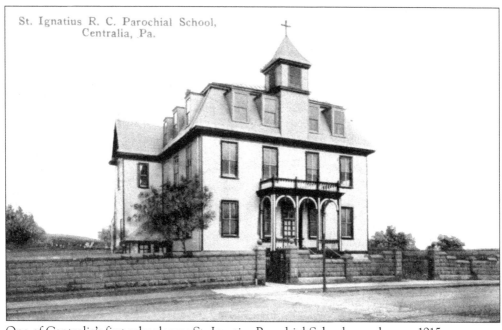

St. Ignatius R. C. Parochial School, Centralia, Pa.

One of Centralia's first schools was St. Ignatius Parochial School, seen here c. 1915.

These north (above) and south views (below) depict Locust Avenue in 1903. A trolley ran from Centralia to Mount Carmel, as evidenced by the tracks in both images.

Pictured is the trolley line between Centralia and Mount Carmel.

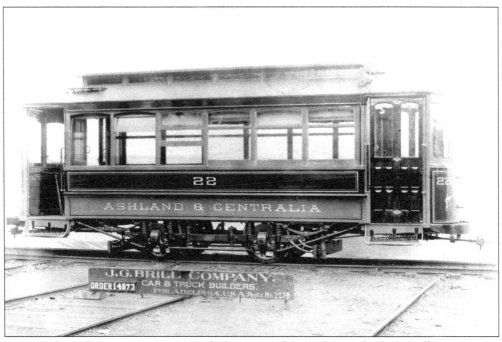

A Centralia trolley car is seen in 1905 before it was delivered from the J. G. Brill Company in Philadelphia. (Courtesy of the Historical Society of Schuylkill County.)

William Hepner (left) was the proprietor of the Centralia House (in operation between 1865 and 1937) until he was murdered in the tavern (below) in 1896.

In this 1894 photograph of the first Centralia fire department, Centralia Hose Company No. 1, president James Davis appears on the hose cart. (Dempsey collection.)

Religious life played an important part in Centralia's history. One of the first churches to be built in town was Holy Trinity Episcopal Church, located on South Locust Avenue. The congregation was organized in 1866. The church was built in 1869 and razed in 1985. The bell from this church is now the Veteran's Monument (see chapter 3).

The very first church built in Centralia was a small sanctuary for the Methodist congregation that had organized in 1866, before the town was incorporated and three years before St. Ignatius Catholic Church was built. In 1886, the bigger Methodist church, pictured *c.* 1912, was constructed on West Center Street.

This 1963 picture depicts how the Methodist church appeared near the time of the beginning of the mine fire.

SS. Peter and Paul Russian Orthodox Church is pictured to the right in 1940 and below in 1966. Note how the classic onion-shaped domes have been replaced following Hurricane Hazel in 1954.

The First English Baptist Church, seen here in 1906, was located on the corner of Troutwine and West Main Streets. The congregation disbanded c. 1917, and the church became a private residence later occupied by the Charles Owen family. (Dempsey collection.)

Do you know whose store this is?
Uncle Frank.

Pictured c. 1906, this general store was built and operated at Locust Avenue and Railroad Street by O. B. Millard and William Shuman in 1865.

These views look south (above) and north (below) down Locust Avenue in 1920.

Locust Avenue (above) and the Neary Hotel and Saloon (below) are decorated for Old Home Week in 1928.

At this local candy store, the sign reads, "Agency for Schrafft's Chocolates—Daintiest of Dainty Sweets."

This photograph was taken near lower Byrnesville, a kind of suburb of Centralia, in 1964.

This image depicts lower Bynesville in 1964.

Locust Avenue is shown here in 1962, the year the fire began.

Built in 1885, Centralia's public school is pictured above in 1913, before it was destroyed by fire in 1935. The new high school, pictured below, was built in 1937 and later renamed Hubert Eicher High School. Centralia merged with the Mount Carmel Area School District in 1963, and the school was closed. The town later sold the building to K-9 Furniture World.

Shown above c. 1963, Izzy Cranzel's Sales Company was located on West Center Street. Below is a photograph of how Centralia appeared in 1964.

Pictured in 1964, this house was, at different times, the residence for the Dempsey, Barrett, and Chapman families.

Although some were aware of the fire, Centralia had a great celebration for its centennial in 1966. Every building pictured here would be torn down in less than 25 years.

This view of Centralia was taken from Paxton Street in 1962, four months after the fire began.

In this 1964 southward view of Locust Avenue, note that the photograph is reversed. The steeple of St. Ignatius Roman Catholic Church appears to be on the left side of the street.

The Centralia Honor Roll was built in observance of those serving in the armed forces.

Centralia Bank, seen here c. 1966, was owned by the Pennsylvania National Bank and Trust Company. (Dempsey collection.)

In this 1977 aerial view of Centralia, St. Ignatius appears at the lower right corner. The street depicted is Locust Avenue, running north to south (top to bottom). (Dempsey collection; courtesy of Alan Klischer.)

Two

Coal Seams
The Mammoth Vein

Centralia rests atop one of the largest veins of anthracite in the country, the Mammoth Vein. The large mining firms were run primarily by the Pennsylvania and Reading railroad companies. Most of the mines were permanently closed in the late 1950s and early 1960s. But they had also been temporarily closed during the Great Depression. The lack of any other type of work in Centralia during this period was disastrous. To get by, Centralians were the first miners in Pennsylvania to start bootlegging coal. The following is one account of those days by native Centralian Harry "Doc" Moleski.

My family has always worked in the mines. If you were a miner, you might go into the mine in almost complete darkness, stand all day and pull the coal out of the vein into a waiting wagon. You only knew that it was full by feeling it with your feet. When the car left the mine, an official would state how much was coal and how much was sludge. The officials often said there was more sludge to cheat the workers inside, and make more profit for the company. Some of the workers went after the men who tried to cheat these poor workers. This is really how the Molly Maguires incident got started in these parts, my father told me. If you were a miner, you were used to terrible conditions, the explosions and cave-ins, and of course death. Every family had someone who was killed in the mines.

You see, I started in the mines at age nine. I used to run long sides the wagon down the tracks as it came out of the mountain to put a piece of wood in the spokes to stop the wagon. It was dangerous work. Mostly, though I tended to the mules, which never ever left the mountain . . . but they were treated good, better than us boys.

When the big mines closed, so many men and families lost their jobs. . . . We would have starved if weren't for the kindnesses of some of the merchants in Centralia, who made sure you had food. If it weren't for Mr. Lippman, who owned the furniture store, my family would have starved. You know, about the only Jewish man in town, but he helped everybody, no matter what their religion.

Many of the miners, like my father, started bootlegging. . . . They would go down in their cellars and break through the foundation 'till they reached a coal vein . . . and you know that the Mammoth Vein runs right through Centralia. So many bootleg mines.

I used to have to crack the coal by hand with a hammer that I would pick up near the stripping pits. I'd go to the grocer and for 10¢ buy the Italian sugar bag. . . . I'd fill them with coal; they were about 400 pounds each, and about 20 bags to a ton. I finally bought a truck in 1938, the first one in these parts (for a bootlegger). I'd drive down to Philadelphia and sell the coal for $8 a bag 'cuz at the breakers they'd only give us $4 a bag. That's if the coal and iron cops didn't catch me. . . . They'd come along and just cut my bags open with a knife and all the coal would just be left at the stripping pit. I'd lose all that time and work breaking up the coal by hand, and the bags.

Mostly, I just remember coming home and telling the family about the food in the restaurants. . . . I never had a hamburger steak until I got my truck and went to Philadelphia. All we ever ate was potatoes and cabbage mostly. Once in a while a pigeon. You cooked everything in one pot. We had potato yeast to make our bread, potato soup, potato jelly, halupski, and our pork and sauerkraut barrel out back of the house. In fact, we never got an icebox till the '30s and an indoor bathroom till '46. We had cardboard for shoes. But we survived, played a lot of knipsy 'cuz we didn't have a radio, couldn't get a station up here on the mountain. But this was home.

The majority of the photographs in this chapter were supplied by former resident, postmaster, and Centralia historian Thomas Dempsey. Dempsey has an extensive free Web site devoted to Centralia, located at http://groups.yahoo.com/group/centcony.

This famous photograph has appeared in many area books about Pennsylvania mining. These workers are inside the North Ashland breaker at Dark Corner in 1890. (Dempsey collection.)

The Girard Trust self-acting coal-loading system, seen here in 1891, was located between Centralia and Big Mine Run in Buck's Patch. (Dempsey collection.)

Mining was a way of life for almost every family in Centralia. Immigrants to the area included Irish, Polish, Slavic, Ukranian, and Portuguese. (Dempsey collection.)

The Centralia Colliery of the Lehigh Valley Coal Company is pictured here in 1928, after the breaker was rebuilt. (Dempsey collection.)

This aerial view of the Mammoth Company stripping pit dates from 1964. (Dempsey collection.)

At the Centralia Colliery in 1891, coal from the Hazel Dell mine was hoisted along the trestle and dumped in the tipple at the top of the breaker. (Dempsey collection.)

The Centralia Colliery appears here 10 years earlier, in 1881. (Dempsey collection.)

These two views depict the Centralia Colliery tipple. (Dempsey collection.)

The shaft and cleaning plant of the Continental Colliery, seen here in 1940, was operated by the Hazlebrook Coal Company. (Dempsey collection; courtesy of Albert S. Miller.)

Shown here is the Lehigh Valley Coal breaker at Centralia. (Dempsey collection.)

Ed Dempsey sits atop the Germantown Colliery fan in 1962. (Dempsey collection.)

Robert Gorrell's colliery was rarely photographed. Gorrell later sold the colliery, and the name was changed to Hazel Dell Colliery, pictured here *c.* 1875. (Dempsey collection.)

The North Ashland breaker, seen here in 1890, was owned by the Philadelphia & Reading Coal and Iron Company. (Dempsey collection.)

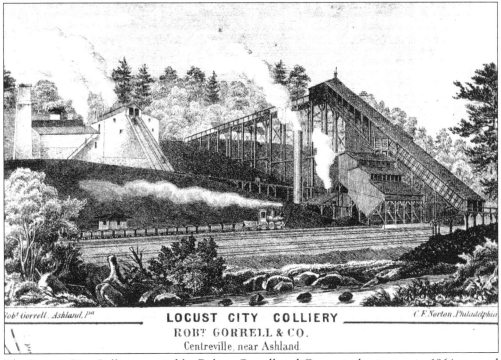

LOCUST CITY COLLIERY
ROBT GORRELL & CO.
Centreville, near Ashland.

The Locust City Colliery, owned by Robert Gorrell and Company beginning in 1864, merged with the Centralia Colliery in the 1880s. (Dempsey collection.)

The Lance Coal Company shop, shown in 1962, was an independent coal company on the old Hazel Dell Colliery. (Dempsey collection.)

Pictured is the drift entrance to the Logan Colliery. (Dempsey collection.)

The Lewis A. Riley and Company Logan Colliery was built in 1880. This image was taken in 1881 by famed Pottsville photographer George M. Bretz. (Dempsey collection.)

The Mammoth Coal Company continental stripping pit is seen here in 1963, at more than 500 feet in depth. Note the shovels in the lower part of the photograph. (Dempsey collection.)

Above, Big Mine Run Plane appears in 1890. Below, the same area is depicted today. Note that, although now obscured by trees, the rock (extreme upper right and below) can be seen in both photographs. (Dempsey collection.)

The Pennsylvania, Lehigh, and Reading railroad companies were major forces in the coal industry. In this rare view of the Logan Colliery, note the train. (Dempsey collection.)

Centralia's railroad depot is pictured at the turn of the century. (Dempsey collection.)

Seen here in April 1963, the Sanchez Construction Company strip mine was located just east of Centralia. (Dempsey collection.)

Workers load timber to be used in the mines. (Dempsey collection.)

This rare view of East Dirt Trip looks south from Buck's Patch. (Dempsey collection.)

Miners prepare to be lowered into the mine. (Dempsey collection.)

The Locust Summit Bagging plant was demolished in 2003. The photograph above was taken in the 1940s, and the photograph below in 1998.

Three

WE THE PEOPLE

The most commonly asked question of Centralia residents is "Why do you choose to live above a mine fire?" The answer I have received begins with the belief that the fire is contained at the top of the hill and really does not threaten the town. In fact, most residents have carbon monoxide detectors in their basements that have not registered any harmful gases in more than a decade. Before she finally moved, Sarah Yeager shared the following story in 1997.

Well, I was born April 16, 1941. And it really didn't register right away. I went through a bout of tuberculosis and I was sick for about 19 months. And when I was in my 30s, I came home and they started talking about the fire and I says, "Where?" And they said, "Behind the Odd Fellows cemetery." Someone was burning trash up there. I said, "What about the bodies up there?" And they said no, it wasn't up there. It was back a little further. This would have been about the early '70s. I'm not sure when they first started talking about leaving. I don't remember until they started getting the fumes and all, and that was around the cemetery. . . . They started offering the big bucks, and a lot of people moved. And I know some of them are sorry they moved. My friends said, "Sarah, don't worry. If we ever move, we'll make sure you get a house next to ours." They moved and never told me. . . .

My great-grandfather built this house. They valued my house in the late '80s and they put that money in escrow in Bloomsburg. They asked to come in again not long ago and look at the house. I let them in to see what they would do. But they really didn't give me any more money. And some of my neighbors wouldn't even let them on their porch. It's supposed to be a voluntary program. But it's not working that way. They want everybody out and they want the coal. . . .

You see, I just don't [know of] any danger. And I was born and raised here in Centralia and I love it. And it's nice; you have friends, you're not real packed in like sardines like we used to. It's like an open country and you don't have people peeking out, seeing what you're doing or who's coming in or out like other places. Many of the neighbors are just like family.

People like Dr. Duffy, our doctor. A big, husky man, but you could go in any time, or call him any time of the day, any time of the night, and he would come down to your house and check you over to see what's wrong. If he had it with him, he'd give you the medicine so you wouldn't have to go to the drugstore and buy it. We paid him, not always in money but in what we had. Chicken, eggs, sewing. He was a wonderful doctor. Or Molly the postmaster. The post office is the place where everyone would meet, standin' on the painwalk out front. And Molly is just about the nicest person you could meet. Every chair in her house said sit down. She always collected money throughout her block if someone was sick, or a family member had died. Every block had someone who collected. One time we had a terrible storm, and the electric was knocked out, some of the tele poles and the power from quite a few homes. Molly brought a kerosene heater for her neighbors so they would have heat. But she never told people that she, too, had no heat. Or Ussie, our Polish leprechaun and drum major at the Legion. He could play the banjo, ukulele, and the harmonica, and could sing up a storm to his rendition of "Give My Regards to Centralia." Then there's Pete's nice Christmas and Fourth of July decorations. Or people sittin' out on Laura Davis's bench.

The people on my block would all bake pies, but on different days, so you could get a fresh piece of pie just about everyday. We shared whatever we had, even if it wasn't very much. I just want people to remember how it was, with everybody getting along without all the drugstores, not the barrooms, all the stores, the merchants, the churches. How your neighbors were your family.

Many of the photographs in this section were supplied by Jerry "Slovie" Wolchansky and the former mayor of Centralia, Anne Marie Devine.

Capt. Jack Crawford, boy soldier, rustic poet, and scout, settled in Centralia in 1861. Later, Crawford served as postmaster of Girardville and fought against the Sioux with Buffalo Bill Cody in the Black Hills. Crawford became a platform speaker and a teller of tales for more than 35 years until his death in 1917. (Courtesy of the Historical Society of Schuylkill County.)

George P. and Catherine M. Lokitis were both born and raised in Centralia. They owned the R & L Coal Company, formerly the Germantown Mine. Their grandson John Lokitis still lives in town.

This cafeteria view was taken by famed Shamokin photographer Paul Thomas in the 1940s.

These candid photographs were taken during World War II.

In the photograph above, three miners take a break. Since Centralia was located on the top of a hill, the temperature could be colder than in Ashland below. Often in the winter, Centralia would be isolated, and people would have to invent their own entertainment, as depicted below.

This girl, perhaps a bit too young to drive, embodies good-natured fun in a small American town.

Abina Sousa is on her way to her First Communion at St. Ignatius.

Joe "Ussie" Shilpetski, pictured to the left, served as the drum major of Centralia's Drum and Bugle Corps from age 18 until the mid-1980s. Below, Ussie is saluted by a young Brian Devine.

Members of the American Legion give a final salute. The American Legion bell once belonged to the Trinity Episcopal congregation.

It was not uncommon to have 9 to 12 people in a family in Centralia.

Bridget and Michael Callahan celebrate as their daughter Mary Ann (Sister Henricho) receives her veil in 1912 from the Sisters of the Immaculate Heart Convent in Centralia. Sister Henricho lived past the age of 90 and was fond of saying, "May St. Patrick give you the green light."

Centralia was very proud of its musical heritage. While St. Ignatius was known for its minstrel shows, Hubert Eicher High School was known for its band.

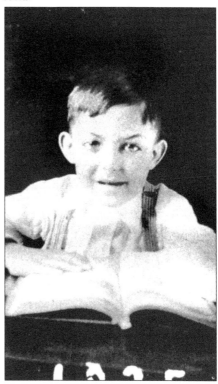

Carl Gray is shown studying in this 1935 photograph.

Centralia had many successful sports teams, as pictured above. Men were not the only basketball stars, as sisters from the Immaculate Heart of Mary demonstrate in the 1980s photograph below. The sisters challenge the children of Mayor Anne Marie Devine.

Friends and classmates enjoy a break before school.

In this 1928 photograph of the Centralia Fire Company, president Michael J. McDonald holds the banner at the center, and to his left is Ed V. Dempsey. (Dempsey collection.)

A Hubert Eicher High School class poses for a photograph.

Tom Hill, Mary Burke-Hill, and Olive R. Hill relax in front of the Country Store and Gas Station *c.* 1951.

Centralia celebrated its quasquicentennial (125 years) in 1991. The king and queen of the parade were Bernie and Molly Darrah, seen riding with Mayor Anne Marie Devine.

Imagine returning for a class reunion where the only part of the town that remains is the memory of you and your classmates.

Ira (left) and Jane (right) help Olive Hill decorate for Christmas in this late-1940s view.

Mary Burke-Hill holds baby Tom Hill while grandmother Olive R. Hill looks on with pride in front of the Country Store and Gas Station in this 1950s photograph.

The Madden Saloon and Hotel, seen here *c.* 1900, was located on the southwest corner of Locust Avenue and East Park Street.

St. Ignatius Parochial School's second-grade class appears in 1956. In the back is Fr. Patrick J. Phalen, who came to Centralia in 1936 and was well known for coordinating minstrel shows. Father Phalen also presided at St. Ignatius' diamond jubilee.

Many of the families in Centralia not only went to school or church together but had been neighbors for several generations. Although other communities in Pennsylvania have had underground mine fires burning longer than 40 years, Centralia was the only community forced to evacuate due to one.

Pictured above are graduates of St. Ignatius Parochial School and their teachers. Below is a classroom in Hubert Eicher High School.

In 1962, when the fire began, Centralia had more than 800 buildings and 1,600 people.

One of the last classes to graduate from Hubert Eicher High School is pictured here.

At one time, Centralia was the only municipality in Pennsylvania in which all the officers were female. Here, Mayor Anne Marie Devine administers the oath of office to Barb Kenenitz, Mary Lou Gaughan, and Molly Darrah. Anne Marie Devine served as mayor of Centralia from 1986 to 1993. Mayor Devine moved from Centralia when Gov. Bob Casey declared eminent domain in Centralia.

These images are courtesy of Jerry "Slovie" Wolchansky. After relocating to Mount Carmel, Slovie returned to Centralia on summer weekends, sharing photographs of what the town used to be like with any visitor or journalist. Until his death, Slovie always maintained that his biggest regret was moving out of Centralia.

Slovie Wolchansky was fond of showing these photographs of students from Hubert Eicher High School (above) and the elementary school (below) to the many visitors to Centralia. He never wanted people to forget about the wonderful town and people that were once here.

Students graduate from Hubert Eicher High School (above) and St. Ignatius Parochial School (below) c. the 1940s.

The marching band from Hubert Eicher High School is shown here.

In the center, Margaret Q. Chapman receives the first relocation check from the Department of Environmental Resources' Nicolas DeBenedictis in 1983.

At one time, Centralia had more than 20 bars within a square mile. One of the most popular was Sousa's.

The owners of Sousa's were John and Irene Sousa, seen to the right. Below, Irene poses with daughter Albina c. 1956.

"Miss Cent____" - 1927

Miss Centralia of 1927, Julia Stanton, is popularly regarded as one of the most beautiful women ever to have lived in Centralia. Julia celebrated her 100th birthday in 2004 by leading her birthday party audience in a rendition of "When Irish Eyes Are Smiling."

Four

THE RISE AND FALL
OF ST. IGNATIUS

Although Centralia had as many as seven churches in its past, St. Ignatius Catholic Church is inextricably tied to the history of the town. First, the town's founder donated the land for the church, choosing a site set on rock so no one coal company would ever disturb the church to mine for coal. Rea's murder, and the role of the Molly Maguires, evoke heated passion. To many of the people in the area, the Mollies were the potential leaders in what would become a union movement for decent wages and safety in the mines. However, the Diocese of Philadelphia sided with the railroad and coal barons, who hired the Pinkerton organization to find the Molly Maguires and prosecute them as murderers and thugs.

St. Ignatius' founding priest, Fr. Daniel J. McDermott, preached against the Mollies from the pulpit of St. Ignatius. This angered many of the residents who saw the Mollies as modern-day Robin Hoods. McDermott was finally reassigned to Philadelphia for his safety. However, a legend began about McDermott. One night, after preaching against the violence attributed to the Mollies and the Ancient Order of Hibernians, McDermott (or his successor) was supposedly beaten up after he refused to stop preaching. Following the beating, he crawled to the church and proclaimed:

> The AOH, Buck Shot, or Molly Maguires, whatever they are called, are a diabolical secret society. Those that belong are a blot and disgrace to the land of their fathers, as well as the land of their adoption. You will all pay for your support of those murderers, the Molly Maguires. I place a curse on all those that are responsible for this crime, on the their families and on their children. One day this town will be erased from the face of the earth. Only the church will stand.

Centralia has had its share of tragedies, and with this momentous fire, rumors of the revenge of the curse began. However, not even St. Ignatius has escaped the destruction and relocation brought about by the fire. In these pages, you will see how this impressive church structure has been a landmark and icon for the town since 1869. You will also see the images from November 1997, when the great church was felled.

At its height, St. Ignatius had more than 3,000 members. The people of Centralia, after working all day in the mines (at least 12-hour shifts), would gather stones from the mountains to help construct the church's foundation. Before St. Ignatius, families such as the Callahans (pictured earlier in this book) would walk down the mountain, more than a mile to nearby Ashland, every day to attend mass. Catholicism was represented by St. Ignatius, and both Russian and Ukranian Orthodox churches, in Centralia.

St. Ignatius was not only a church, but a parochial school and a convent for the Sisters of the Immaculate Heart of Mary. During its first 100 years, St. Ignatius gave more than 18 priests and 35 sisters to the service of the church.

In most images of Centralia, it is the steeple of St. Ignatius that rises from the highest point of the town. In this chapter, you will see the church from drawings in the 1870s until the steeple was torn down on Thanksgiving weekend in 1997.

One of the oldest graves in St. Ignatius cemetery belongs to Fr. Michael C. Power. St. Ignatius reached its full flower under him, with more than 3,000 parishioners. Six thousand people attended his funeral in 1895. According to the *Diocese of Harrisburg: 1868–1968*, Bishop Thomas McGovern stated in his eulogy, "Father Power was a man with a soul divine, charitable and kind to all. . . . His name calls forth praise and found recollection."

St. IGNATIUS Roman Catholic Church · Centralia, Columbia Co. Penna.
Rev. E. T. FIELD PASTOR

This 1876 rendition of St. Ignatius mistakenly places the convent on the left instead of the right side of the church.

The St. Ignatius church (right) and rectory (below) are shown as they appeared in 1944.

These pages reveal front and back views of the St. Ignatius church, rectory, and convent. This image dates from 1944.

This photograph of St. Ignatius was taken a few days before the church was demolished in 1997.

In this postcard view of St. Ignatius, notice the trolley tracks.

This image of the St. Ignatius buildings is one of the last before they were razed.

The convent and rectory of St. Ignatius were torn down years before the church was demolished.

St. Ignatius stood alone for many years, as the rectory and convent were demolished first.

The altar area of St. Ignatius appears just before destruction in 1997. Scattered on the ground are bulletins from the last service.

The night before the steeple was torn down, an ice storm coated the trees, making the church glisten in the sun. Notice how the cross remains atop the steeple, as attempts to remove it had been unsuccessful.

During Thanksgiving weekend in 1997, the steeple, one of Centralia's most enduring icons, was demolished.

Only five people witnessed the demolition. Many felt that it would have been too painful to watch.

The front wall of St. Ignatius was the last to fall.

A roofless St. Ignatius begins to disappear.

Today, only a small planter marks the spot where St. Ignatius stood for more than 100 years.

Five

THE FIRE DOWN BELOW
DEMOLITION AND RELOCATION

The fire broke out during Memorial Day weekend in 1962 just north of the Odd Fellows cemetery. It all started when the town, as practiced annually, burned trash in an abandoned mine shaft. On May 22, 1969, the first three families were moved from Centralia. One failed attempt to put out the fire included digging a trench and using fly ash and clay seal. According to Renee Jacobs, author of *Slow Burn: A Photo Document of Centralia, Pennsylvania*, the attempt had been $50,000 short of completion. Jacobs suggests that if workers had continued to dig for three shifts nonstop and not stopped to open bids for the rest of the job, Centralia may have been saved.

Later, in the early 1980s, young Todd Domboski fell into a hole that opened under him 4 feet wide and 150 feet deep. He clung to an exposed tree root and was pulled to safety by his cousin. Government officials were across the street when the boy was rescued, and soon a plan hatched for a federal volunteer buyout of the town. By 1983, the government said the fire was advancing on three or four fronts. Proposed trenching would have cost $660 million and may not have worked. The town voted 345 to 200 to accept a government buyout. Some $7 million had been spent up to 1984, and the buyout added another $42 million. The entire process is chronicled in such books as David DeKok's *Unseen Danger: A Tragedy of People, Government, and the Centralia Mine Fire* and J. Stephen Kroll-Smith's and Stephen Robert Couch's *The Real Disaster is above Ground: A Mine Fire & Social Conflict*.

By the early 1990s, Gov. Bob Casey had declared eminent domain, and the voluntary buyout thus became mandatory. Governor Casey purportedly stated he "did not want to be awakened one night by a tragedy in Centralia that could have been prevented." Many of the remaining 50 residents moved after this declaration. The choice to move or stay sometimes pitted neighbor against neighbor. It also separated families that had been neighbors for generations.

In one horrific incident, a man told his wife that they were leaving, and she refused. After terrible pressure, he killed her, drove to the top of the mountain, and doused himself with gasoline, committing suicide. Many of the remaining residents moved during the 1990s, citing the stress of not knowing when the state might move in to evict them.

But why would someone stay in a town on fire? One common misconception regarding the Centralia Mine Fire is that flames threatened the town. During the first 20 years of the fire, occasional brush fires occurred due to the heat. No one, however, has ever reported seeing flames. However, a popular story in Centralia centers on how a visiting newspaper crew, disappointed with the lack of a visible fire, set a newspaper aflame and photographed the result.

The press has in fact had a love affair with Centralia. *Time, Newsweek,* the *New York Times,* CBS, CNN, the *London Times,* the Australian Broadcasting Network, and German Television are just a few of the more than 200 news outlets that have covered this story. ABC's *Nightline with Ted Kopple* even did a live remote broadcast from the town. Although officially discouraged by the state of Pennsylvania, journalists and curious travelers visit Centralia daily.

Some people believe that the fire is not still burning. They believe what is seen are the remnants from the heated rock below. Others believe there is a fire and that there is enough coal below ground to burn for 1,000 years. Officially, the town's residents are considered guests of the state of Pennsylvania, not owners of their own homes. No one is allowed to sell or rent their property, since the state legally owns the land.

Centralia sits directly over one of the largest veins of anthracite in the nation. Some residents refused to move, thinking the state just wanted to get at the coal under the town. The borough of Centralia in fact sued the state in the 1990s to be compensated for the coal if and when it was ever harvested. The Supreme Court of Pennsylvania found that in this case of eminent domain, the rights to coal belonged to the state.

An attempt to find a common site for relocation resulted in an area called New Centralia, which attracted only a few residents. Centralia, a community of 1,600 in 1962, has now dwindled to just 10 today.

The first attempt to extinguish the Centralia Mine Fire, in 1962, stopped when the money ran out. By the time a new bid for the job was accepted, the fire had spread to a point that the government was never able to put out. (Dempsey collection.)

View of Centralia, Pa. From The Centralia Colliery....1962

This aerial view of Centralia was taken in 1962, when the fire began. (Dempsey collection.)

People expecting to see giant flames in Centralia are always disappointed. Here, a rare fire has broken the surface and ignited brush.

The most common visual evidence of the fire is the steam and gas escaping to the surface. Since hot air rises, the view of the gases is always more prevalent in the colder months.

These photographs were taken in December 1997. In addition to the steam, a very strong smell of sulfur is present. Notice the pipe venting the underground gases in the photograph below. Near this area, the author recorded a temperature of 800 degrees just 12 inches below the surface.

These two images represent the most visible aspects of the fire. The area is near the former site of Hubert Eicher High School.

This area is adjacent to the St. Ignatius cemetery and the cemetery of SS. Peter and Paul. The gas is not as visible during the summer months.

This foglike steam has a strong odor of sulfur. Some visitors to the area complain not only of the smell but of headaches after touring the area.

These photographs were taken near the former site of St. Ignatius. Alexander Rea donated the land for St. Ignatius because it was on solid rock.

Shown here is evidence of the fire on the hill that leads to Ashland.

The money for relocation was received in the fall of 1983. Most of the relocation and demolition thus occurred between 1984 and 1986.

Little time was wasted in removing the houses once they were vacated.

Since this was originally a volunteer program, some homeowners remained as their neighbor's home was destroyed.

In 1986–1987, the Hemdale Film Corporation filmed the boarded-up main street homes in Centralia for the feature film *Made in America*, starring Christopher Penn.

One family that refused to move had to endure a harsh winter with no outside wall for several months after their neighbor's row house was torn down.

Although heavy equipment could be used to tear down most buildings (as these two photographs illustrate), some row homes had to be dismantled by hand as not to cause the adjoining structure to collapse.

The buildings in these pictures had stood for over 100 years.

The flavor of Wrigley's gum may last a long, long time, but this building was not as lucky.

Six

GIVE MY REGARDS TO OLD CENTRALIA

40 YEARS OF LIVING WITH FIRE

With the exception of seemingly abandoned streets, today Centralia resembles its origins in 1841 more than a town in the 21st century. Recently, the state of Pennsylvania has discontinued the mowing of the numerous properties they own. The result is that vegetation and wildlife have flourished. Deer, turkeys, and other birds now populate the area around Centralia. Even the occasional bear has been seen walking down an empty road. Now, fewer than 20 of the almost 800 buildings remain, and the few residents still live in fear—not of the fire, but of a day when the state may physically remove them from their homes.

When I began venturing to Centralia to gather information for a play about the fire, I did not expect to find a place so rich. I discovered a town rich in history, in colorful stories, and people rich with generosity. The focus of my play, and now this book of images, is to try to capture a part of the richness of Centralia, a town where your neighbors are your family—arguments and all.

In a recent series of articles for the *Times-Shamrock,* writer Robyn Meadows wrote that Centralia is "a tiny town where people still cling to an old way of life when a person's home was his or her castle and no one had the right to take it away." The passion and nostalgia for a time and a community now past has been communicated to me by every current and former Centralia resident I have met. I first went to Centralia in 1997.

People ask me why I continue to return to the area. My answer is simply that I have found the people of this area among the friendliest and most generous people I know. When I wrote my play about Centralia, people donated and lent me original clothing and artifacts from throughout the town's history. The people offered unconditional friendship and trust.

On one of my first visits to Centralia, people were returning from the funeral of Joe "Ussie" Shilpetski. Ussie was known as "the Polish leprechaun," and his photograph appears in chapter 3.

I was told that Ussie often grabbed his ukulele, walked into the middle of the street, and stopped traffic to sing "Give My Regards to Old Centralia." Ussie's words best sum up the feelings and images that many of the Centralians have shared with me.

Oh, Give my regards to Centralia
Remember me to Phillip Lippman's Square,
Tell all the boys up at Coddington's Gassie
And Hose House I'll be there.

Tell 'em at Puddin' Reilley's
I miss the poker games played there,
Give my regards to Centralia
My hometown in despair.

Remember swimmin' in the old Breaker Dam
Or skatin' on the old Duck Pond?
The sheeney, the bucksters, the umbrella-man
Had a very special bond.

Green leaves were five for a penny
Pepsi was a nickel worth a dime,
Three cents was the price of an ice cream cone
Oh what a joy to hear those bells chime.

Good-bye to Hinchey's Night Club
Jack McGinley's Hotel,
Good-bye to Zimbo's, Mekosh's & Gaughan's
Many stories were there to tell.

So long McCullion's and Muldowney's
Wolchansky's and Sousa's, too,
Don't forget old Smokey's Distillery
And that old-fashioned brew.

Give my regards to Centralia
Remember me to the Old Town Square
Tell all the boys up at Coddington's Gassie
And Hosey I'll be there.

Tell them at the Legion
I miss the drum and bugle corps,
Tell all my friends up on Paxton Street
Wish I could be their neighbor once more.

Give my regards to Centralia
She's in my heart and prayers!

This bench looks upon the memorial to the former site of the American Legion.

The Assumption Beloved Virgin Mary (BVM) Church, known as St. Mary's, resides on the hill overlooking Centralia. Though technically not within township limits, this is the only one of Centralia's seven churches still standing and active.

These warning signs first appeared in Centralia in April 1998. They read, "Walking or driving in this area could result in serious injury or death. Dangerous gases are present. Ground is prone to sudden collapse." There are, however, no fences to restrict visitors.

The pipes in these photographs, known as bore holes, were designed to vent the gases from the mine fire below. They are surrounded by fencing, and people throw bottles and cans inside to watch how the escaping heat will melt the trash.

This block was once crowded with row homes.

Current and former residents of Centralia are often found sitting and reminiscing about the town on summer weekends. The sign is a heart that reads, "We Love Centralia." The heart and several benches have been stolen, replaced, and stolen again as souvenirs.

On this corner of Locust at Park, Alexander Rea's residence once stood. Some of the brick fencing from his 1866 home still remains.

This photograph was taken from the abandoned basketball courts, where Centralia's sports teams played.

The borough hall is the only government building remaining. It houses Centralia's fire truck and ambulance, which is mainly staffed by volunteers from neighboring Aristes. Beginning in the late 1990s, Centralians have not been allowed to pay property taxes, since the state of

Pennsylvania officially owns their homes. Thus, there is not a local tax base to maintain the fire department, the Hose House, or "Hosey," as it is called in the coal region.

This present-day view looks north on Locust Avenue. Although the area was once crowed with homes, people driving through are sometimes unaware they are in Centralia.

In this southward view of Locust Avenue, the vacant land is the former site of St. Ignatius.

Route 61 was permanently rerouted when repeated repairs to the road failed to stop the pavement from cracking and splitting open.

This view shows an abandoned section of Route 61.

The St. Ignatius cemetery borders the most visible sites of the mine fire. A visitor to his father's grave once remarked to the author, "My father always wanted to be cremated, but when my father died the Catholic Church wouldn't allow it. Now I guess he'll get his wish."

Former Centralia resident Tom Hill keeps the memory of the town alive with his racecar, the "Centralia Flash."

In the distance is the solitary house of the mayor of Centralia, Lamar Mervine.

Now in his late 80s, lifelong resident Lamar Mervine has been mayor of Centralia since 1993. When asked why he stayed, he replied, "This is the only home I've ever known."

Printed in the USA
CPSIA information can be obtained
at www.ICGtesting.com
LVHW081957120923
757853LV00009B/593